Designer Dogs

Morkie

A Cross between a Maltese and a Yorkshire Terrier

by Heather E. Schwartz

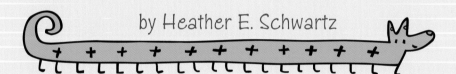

Consultant:

Tanya Dewey, PhD

University of Michigan Museum of Zoology

Ann Arbor, Michigan

CAPSTONE PRESS
a capstone imprint

Snap Books are published by Capstone Press,
1710 Roe Crest Drive, North Mankato, Minnesota 56003.
www.capstonepub.com

 Books published by Capstone Press are manufactured with paper
containing at least 10 percent post-consumer waste.

Library of Congress Cataloging-in-Publication Data
Schwartz, Heather E.
 Morkie : a cross between a Maltese and a Yorkshire terrier / by Heather Schwartz.
   p. cm.—(Snap. Designer dogs)
 Includes bibliographical references and index.
 Summary: "Describes Morkies, their characteristics and behavior, and includes basic information on feeding, grooming, training, and
health care"—Provided by publisher.
 ISBN 978-1-4296-7668-7 (library binding)
 1. Morkie—Juvenile literature. I. Title.
SF429.M67S39 2012
 636.76—dc23   2011036699

Editorial Credits
Editor: Lori Shores
Designer: Veronica Correia
Media Researcher: Marcie Spence
Photo Stylist: Sarah Schuette
Studio Scheduler: Marcy Morin
Production Specialist: Kathy McColley

Photo Credits:
Capstone Studio: Karon Dubke, cover (top), 5, 6, 7, 8 (left), 9 (top), 13, 15, 17, 18, 19, 20, 21, 23, 25, 26, 27, 29; Shutterstock: Eric
Isselee, cover (bottom both), 8 (right), Felix Mizioznikov, 11, Konstantin Gushcha, 10, Natalia Kuznetsova, 9 (bottom)

Printed in the United States of America in North Mankato, Minnesota.
102011   006405CGS12

Table of Contents

Chapter 1

Introducing the Morkie

Morkies are small dogs that pack plenty of personality. Some people say Morkies are great watchdogs even though they're little. They're quick to bark if they sense trouble, and they seem fearless. Most Morkies are also friendly. They're loving and loyal to their human families.

Look around and you might spot a Morkie anywhere. Since they're only about the size of a football, many owners tote them around town. A Morkie peeking out of a ladies' handbag may look like a cute accessory. But that's not why Morkies are called designer dogs.

Not Really Toys

Morkies are sometimes called teacup or toy dogs because they're tiny. But some breeders purposely breed dogs that are too small. These names might be cute, but dogs that are too small can be unhealthy.

What Is a Designer Dog?

Morkie

A designer dog is a cross between two **purebred** dogs. Morkies and other designer dogs are also called crossbreed dogs. Morkies are part Yorkshire Terrier and part Maltese. Breeders try to create puppies with the best qualities of both parent **breeds**. Many Morkies are less nervous than their Yorkie parent, for example. But unlike purebreds, designer dogs often look quite different from each other. For this reason, the American Kennel Club (AKC) does not recognize them as true breeds. The AKC sets standards for size, appearance, and personality of purebred dogs.

Sometimes designer dogs are bred for specific reasons. Labradoodles are a cross between Labrador retrievers and poodles. They were created when a breeder needed a guide dog that didn't shed. Some breeders say crossbreed dogs may be healthier than purebreds. These breeders believe some health problems may be avoided by crossbreeding. Other designer dogs are bred simply to be good pets.

purebred—having parents of the same breed
breed—a certain kind of animal within an animal group; breed also means to mate and raise a certain kind of animal

Labradoodle

Chapter 2

Barking Up the Family Tree

As a designer dog, the Morkie is a new breed. But their purebred parents have a long history. The Maltese's origins can be traced back thousands of years. This breed hasn't changed much over time. They're small dogs weighing between 4 to 9 pounds (1.8 to 4 kilograms.) Their white hair is long and silky. Like many small dogs, Maltese can have problems with their eyes, ears, and knees. But Maltese have personalities that have made them popular for centuries. They are lively and fearless but gentle and loving too.

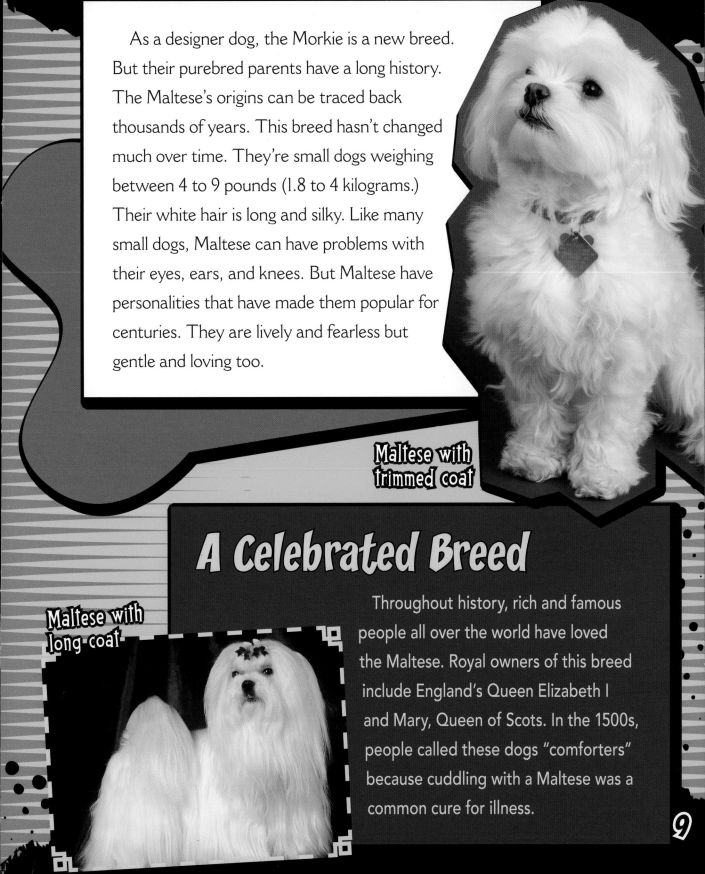

Maltese with trimmed coat

A Celebrated Breed

Maltese with long coat

Throughout history, rich and famous people all over the world have loved the Maltese. Royal owners of this breed include England's Queen Elizabeth I and Mary, Queen of Scots. In the 1500s, people called these dogs "comforters" because cuddling with a Maltese was a common cure for illness.

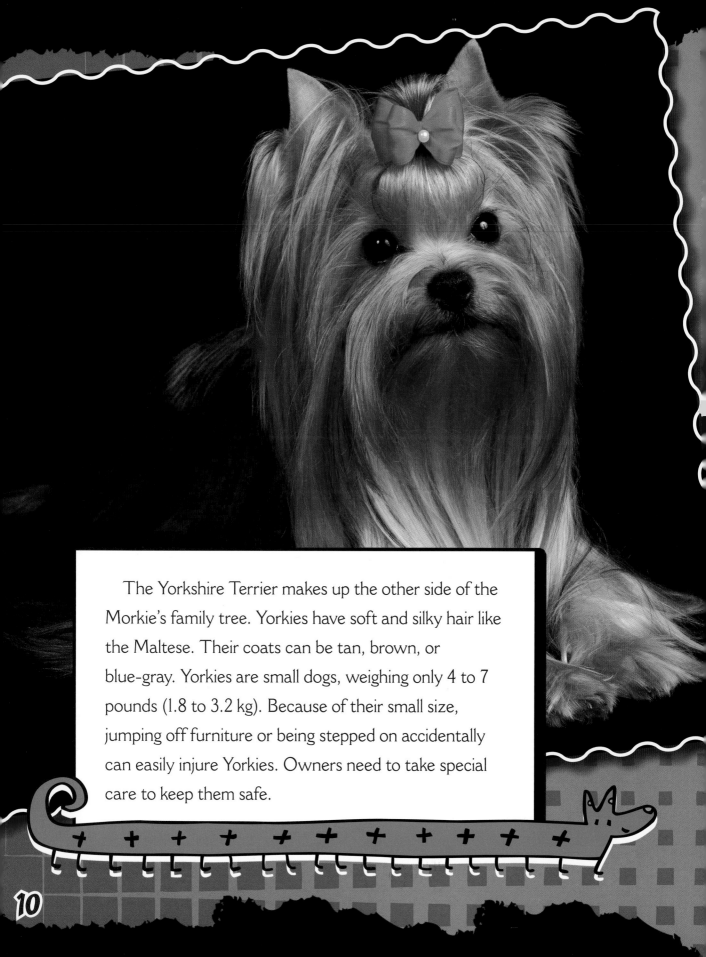

The Yorkshire Terrier makes up the other side of the Morkie's family tree. Yorkies have soft and silky hair like the Maltese. Their coats can be tan, brown, or blue-gray. Yorkies are small dogs, weighing only 4 to 7 pounds (1.8 to 3.2 kg). Because of their small size, jumping off furniture or being stepped on accidentally can easily injure Yorkies. Owners need to take special care to keep them safe.

While their appearance is striking, the Yorkie's **temperament** may be why this breed is popular. Yorkies are brave, energetic, and playful. But they're also affectionate with their owners. They are loyal dogs that want to protect their owners.

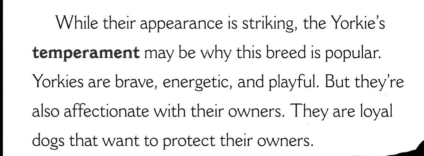

Dogs with Jobs

Yorkies were brought to Yorkshire, England, from Scotland during the mid-1800s. Unlike the pampered Maltese, Yorkies started out as working-class dogs. Weavers kept Yorkies to catch rats in their clothing mills.

temperament—the combination of an animal's behavior and personality

Chapter 3

A Pretty Pleasing Pet

There is no guarantee that a Morkie will have all the desired **traits** from their parent breeds. Some Morkies have the pointy ears of a Yorkshire Terrier. Others have ears that hang down Maltese-style. However, most Morkies do look alike. They're small dogs like their parents. Their long, soft coats may be brown, tan, white, black, or a combination of colors. Most Morkies are smaller and lighter than a gallon of milk. They stand about 8 to 10 inches (20 to 25 centimeters) tall and weigh just 3 to 7 pounds (1.4 to 3.2 kg).

trait— a quality or characteristic that makes one person or animal different from another

Dog Fact!

Morkies are
sometimes called
Yorktese or Malkies.

FEISTY, FUN AND FEARLESS

Morkies get a mix of personality traits from their parents too. Like Maltese, they're cute, cuddly lap dogs. They need plenty of attention from their owners, much like Yorkshire Terriers. Morkies are usually friendlier with other pets than Yorkies. They'll even rush to greet animals they've never met before.

Morkies have lots of energy. They need space to run, but not as much as larger dogs. A small yard provides plenty of room for these little dogs to get exercise. Morkies love to play, but rough play isn't a good idea. Morkies can be easily hurt because they're so small. Families with young children need to supervise playtime with a Morkie.

Chapter 4

Caring for a Morkie

Visiting the Vet

Like all dogs, Morkies need regular checkups and **vaccinations**. Seeing a veterinarian regularly can also help catch health problems. Some Morkies develop issues with their knees or eyes like their purebred parents. The vet will also check your Morkie's teeth. Small dogs often have dental problems. Some owners brush their dogs' teeth. Others use dental treats made just for dogs. The vet can help you decide what is best for your dog.

vaccination—a shot of medicine that protects animals from a disease

FEEDING

Morkies eat two to four meals each day because they burn energy quickly. Dog food made for small dogs will be the right size for their miniature mouths. Wet food is sometimes easier to digest, while dry food can help keep teeth clean. Your vet can help you decide which type of food is best. Whatever you choose, be sure to feed your dog the same food every day. And remember that people food is not good for dogs. Changes in diet can upset a Morkie's stomach.

GET GROOMING

Morkies shed very little. But like all dogs, Morkies need to be groomed. Every day, the hair around their eyes should be cleaned with a wet cloth. Morkies also need daily brushing to keep their hair from getting **mats**. Give your Morkie a bath with dog shampoo every two or three weeks. Their short legs keep them close to the ground, so they get dirty easily. But bathing a Morkie too often can dry out its skin.

Morkies also need their nails clipped. Clippers made specifically for dogs work well for regular trimming. However, it's best to let an adult handle nail clipping. It can be difficult to keep the dog still and cut the nails properly. If a dog's nails are cut too short, they can bleed and be painful.

mat—a thick, tangled mess of hair

To Groom or Not to Groom?

For many Morkie owners, grooming is a chance to spend some quiet time with their pet. Not everyone feels comfortable trimming fur or nails, though. Some owners take their Morkies to a groomer instead. The vet can also step in when necessary. Sometimes dogs need professional teeth cleaning or other dental procedures.

Morkies are smart dogs that can learn many tricks. Some Morkies even learn to use a litter box. But first, teach your Morkie basic commands, such as sit, stay, and come. This basic **obedience training** will keep your pet safe. For example, if your dog races off after a squirrel, you can shout, "Come!" Instead of running into the street, your dog should return to you.

When your Morkie responds to a command correctly, offer a reward right away. Also be sure to praise your dog for a job well done. Some dogs do better with food rewards, and others like play or attention as rewards. For Morkies, treats, praise, play, and petting are all great rewards.

obedience training—teaching an animal to obey commands

Beyond Training

Even if your dog is trained to stay by your side, there's more you can do to keep your Morkie safe.

↪ Use a leash when you leave home. Morkies are so friendly, they're likely to leave your side to greet other dogs. Some of those dogs may not be as nice. Morkies might also run away if they're frightened or want to chase other animals.

↪ Make sure your Morkie wears a collar. It should be small and light, so it will fit comfortably and won't slip off. Attach a tag with your name, address, and phone number on it.

↪ Most cities also require your dog to be licensed. A dog license can help you find your pet if it becomes lost.

BAD DOG?

Sometimes Morkies misbehave. They might chew on furniture or bark for no reason at all. Does that mean you have a bad dog? Not necessarily. Many dogs behave badly when they're bored, lonely, or frustrated. It's their way of telling you they need more attention, exercise, or toys. Some extra training can also help control unwanted behaviors.

When you're trying to stop bad behavior, make sure you're not rewarding it. When owners yell at a barking dog, they're rewarding the dog with attention. Sometimes people pet a barking dog to calm it. But really, they're rewarding the dog for barking. It's better to take another approach. Some owners ignore the noise and reward the dog when it stops barking.

Don't be discouraged if training takes a while. Helping your Morkie master new skills takes time and patience. You'll be successful if you are consistent with your training and encourage your dog rather than showing frustration. Besides, all that practicing is wonderful bonding time for you and your pet.

The W-A-L-K

A great cure for a bored dog is a simple walk. Regular walks are great exercise. They also satisfy a dog's curiosity by letting it see and smell new things. Because Morkies are small dogs, they will get tired on a long walk. Keep walks to a few blocks, and choose a different direction each time. Then your Morkie can see and smell new things every time you go out.

Chapter 5

Adopting a Morkie

Most people know dogs aren't meant to be accessories. Responsible dog owners do their homework before adopting. They research which breed will fit best with their family. They learn about the type of care different dogs need. They make good choices to find a pet that will match their lifestyle.

Morkies typically don't like to be alone. They love attention and meeting new people. That makes them great companions for owners who are home a lot. But they're also great pets for owners who can take them along on trips. While Morkies can be excitable, they tend to travel well. Morkies generally calm down when they're held and petted.

If you think a Morkie would fit into your family, there are many ways to find one. Check rescue organizations and animal shelters first. Morkies are popular dogs, but sometimes they end up in shelters. If you don't find one, ask a local veterinarian for help in finding a breeder.

Good breeders raise happy and healthy dogs. The dogs spend time in the house and have a clean outdoor area to run. Good breeders can tell you about the health of their puppies and the puppies' parents. They even offer a health guarantee for adopted pets.

Bad News Breeders

Puppy mills are places where large numbers of puppies are bred, but the animals are not cared for properly. Often the parent dogs live in terrible conditions. You can report breeders you suspect of mistreating their animals by calling your local Humane Society. Walk away if a breeder exhibits these warning signs:

- doesn't seem to know much about the breed offered
- has puppies available all the time
- won't let you see the area where dogs are kept
- won't let you meet the puppies' mother

FINDING YOUR DOG

No matter where you find a Morkie, spend some time with the dog before bringing it home. Make sure it seems lively, friendly, and happy. That's a sign it's been raised properly. Also consider the energy level of the puppy. Some puppies are more energetic than others. Most people are better off with a puppy that is neither too excitable nor too shy.

You'll also want to determine what temperament you're looking for in your new pet. Some Morkies can be timid and withdrawn. Others are outgoing and curious. Watch the puppies to see how they act with each other. Ask questions about the puppies' health and personality. That's how you'll find the best dog for you.

Adopting a Morkie is a big commitment. But taking good care of a pet shows love and respect for the animal. It's a big responsibility, but Morkie owners agree it's worth the effort. For all the love and care you give your dog, you'll be rewarded with as much love and loyalty from your Morkie.

Should You Adopt a Morkie?

Answer the following questions honestly. The more times you answer yes, the more likely a Morkie is right for you.

1. Do you have time to brush a pet every day?
2. Is your home or yard big enough for a small dog to run and play?
3. If your family is active, can you bring a little dog along when you're on the go?
4. Do you want a pet that doesn't shed too much?
5. Do you have the patience to train a dog?

Glossary

breed (BREED)—a certain kind of animal within an animal group; breed also means to mate and raise a certain kind of animal

mat (MAT)—a thick, tangled mess of hair

obedience training (oh-BEE-dee-uhns TRAY-ning)—teaching an animal to obey commands purebred (PYOOR-bred)—having parents of the same breed

purebred (PYOOR-bred)—having parents of the same breed

temperament (TEM-pur-uh-muhnt)—the combination of an animal's behavior and personality; the way an animal usually acts or responds to situations shows its temperament

trait (TRATE)—a quality or characteristic that makes one person or animal different from another

vaccination (vak-suh-NAY-shun)—a shot of medicine that protects animals from a disease

Read More

Gagne, Tammy. *Yorkshire Terriers.* All about Dogs. Mankato, Minn.: Capstone Press, 2010.

Palika, Liz. *Dog Obedience: Getting Your Pooch Off the Couch and Other Dog Training Tips.* Dog Ownership. Mankato, Minn.: Capstone Press, 2012.

Stone, Lynn M. *Maltese.* Eye to Eye with Dogs. Vero Beach, Fla.: Rourke Pub., 2009.

Internet Sites

FactHound offers a safe, fun way to find Internet sites related to this book. All of the sites on FactHound have been researched by our staff.

Here's all you do:

Visit *www.facthound.com*

Type in this code: 9781429676687

Super-cool stuff! Check out projects, games and lots more at www.capstonekids.com

31

Index